Xilla Club

www.xilla.club

The Great Stock Market Roast

The Great Stock Market Roast

2019 -2020

The Stock Market Roast

Nobody spared. Not Trump. Not Alan Greenspam.

Yeah. He spammed the markets. So there you go.

Quotes for the Recession

Quotes and Last Thoughts For Being So Dumb.

Take it with a pinch of salt or take it with red chilli. It's that spicy.

Nothin' is great about 2019-20 is great. Except the crash.

From here to Economic Armageddon we will be here with you fight with you all d way, watch helplessly as stocks crumble, PE enter single digits, and of course we will be with you when you hit the pub and say 1 down and 3 to go. But don't worry we will let you on to a little secret. Just as we told you it's going to crash we already know there will be a revival.

Read All about it in The Last Thoughts & Spicy Quotes

For The Great Stock Market Meltdown Of the Century. Ladieees N Gentlemen. Live.

The ship is going to sink. We might as well enjoy the swim as we go down.

Ha Ha Ha Ha

It's time to point your finger.

Ok Ok. Go Ahead.

But I meant it's time to point your index finger and say- He said that! And see what happened.

But then we have Quotes- Analytic, poignant, scathingly brutal, really truthful, some so predictive almost prophetic, some funny and all very unique and striking. To all these add your own, mix some wit, sarcasm and emoticon and forward to each other on your favorite apps, come on television if you can, go on radio broadcast or web podcast and use all these quotes to brighten up the evenings when you day has been butchered by the falling stocks whose bottom seems to be so large and without end.

The tiger grows cat's whiskers

And it doesn't want to let on. But hell!
The Emperor wears no clothes; but no
one wants to let it on!

Trump or a trumpet..huh!

It's easy to win the trade war if not for
Powell!

It's easy to win a trade war if not for the
Fed.

I wish I hadn't fired the former chair.

Trade wars are so easy, if Powell hadn't
meddled. He started it all. No it was the
Brexit.

Nay Nay it was Alan Greenspan.

Who's that...?

What did Alan Greenspan get Right when he presided over the housing bubble episode?

People's poor memory with names. They would forget it all.

What did Alan Greenspan do? He spammed the markets and got away with it.

Why not call him Greenspam.

When Greenspam was the head, the bubble was growing all around him. He now says ' I didn't know' (And he's written a book based on – I don't know****!!)

You are the principal o' a school. N you don't know the alphabet. Kids will laugh at you maan.

No ones to blame. It's just the cycles.

What?

Bank frauds are no big deal. They are routine.

CEO's deserve to earn in hundreds of millions. They deserve it.

Extrapolate that – the poor don't deserve.

Extrapolate that – Investors deserve a market meltdown

Twitter Twitter Who's the favorite of them all. Trump Trump

Jump Jump where no one wants to tread

Lead us kindly to redemptiom. Ppppp Ppppp.

I want to fire. Fire in the air, fire above the wall, fire Powell, fire everyone.

 Fire in the well run run run...

I am bright and beautiful. I'm the chosen one.

And the All Time Great Quote

There can be not be another financial crisis........ in our life time.

Take a guess Who Said That?

(Clue - It came from the Fed).

Xilla Says – There have been 33 recessions. There will be another one.

The Last Thoughts

A falling value pinches everyone. A tiger grows cat's whiskers.

China is much much weaker than it lets on. Slow growth, huge debt. Drudging weight on global economy.

The indicators are the result.

Be humane. Don't rip off your own customers.

Zero interest rate regimes has led to over-production.

A consumption not driven by need contributes to the formation of a bubble.

That economy which circulates within reasonable limits spikes within reasonable limits. And the economy which crosses all limits crashes without limit.

Wal-Mart, Macys, Sears close hundreds of stores laying of tens of thousands of workers.

Search for places to hide. To escape the avalanche of the economic downswing.

Live at the fringe. Get the best of both the worlds.

Live at the fringe. Get the best of the forest and get away from the worst of the city.

Trump. Trade wars And The Great Fall Of China.

Chinese real estate magnate Wang Jianlin has stated that "Residential real estate in China is now the biggest bubble in history." One prick and the blast will wipe off a third of GDP.

Torsten Slok who works as a chief international economist has a chart which shows that China's credit bubble exceeded even that of USA on the edge of subprime mortgage meltdown that led into the 2008 recession.

Mar 2017: China central bank head states the China debt is a huge concern and they must bring it down quickly. China debt is 300 %

(Debt/GDP)

All this without a trade war.

If a trade war starts? Absolute Terror.

South China Sea and the domination streak of China.

China aspires to be the world leader. By means fair and not so fair. Times Up.

We will have ample time to think about this as the events unfold before our seemingly unbelieving eyes.

Even if China does compromise in the trade war then it compromises its own economy and that's still bad news for the globe.

The culprits are the banks. They give 'easy' money. And expect it back.

Did the banks think that people will borrow from them and make profits out of a tentative economy?

It will begin with the banks. And extend everywhere.

Uninvest to Reinvest.

Banks or casinos?

When banks become casinos the economy is a gamble.

The moon is a safe place. I will go there. Because there are no banks on the moon.

The stats are staggeringly negative.

The Stoxx last reached its high in 2000. Since then it has been hitting lower highs.

Right now the Stoxx has formed a shoulder-head-shoulder pattern.

And the projection is a lower high and a lower high.

The signals from Eurozone are the color Red.

Europe will be the straw that broke the camel's back.

Europe is as brittle as an old woman's grey hair.

QE: When everything fails we fall back on magic. Close your eyes. Open now. Hey we have more money ! The voodoo economics of the voodoo economists.

Be brave and bite the bullet. We should have. The last chance was missed.

The End Result is an extrapolation of the initial decision multiplied by a factor.

The End Result is Upon Us.

This time the recession will teach us to be humane.

To purge the wild excesses, the panicky decisions, the irrational behavior, the greedy clinging and the selfish motivations and cowardly attitude.

Be ready for fly by wire decisions.

There will be minimal government intervention. Coz governments have done all they could. And have no more tricks in the bag.

Nature has given us many years and more opportunities to take effective action. But when we don't, it steps in and makes sure we pay for the economic blunders we have committed.

We have a downswing. Look up. Someone up there may know what he is doing. Read 'The King And The Preacher' in The Sign Of The Bear.

Marks And Spencer shuts down a 100 stores. A 100...!!!

15 Nov 2016. French PM: "Europe on brink of Collapse." We are here now...

When the indicators are bad the result cannot be good.

Economic indicators are like health indicators. When you have a bad lab test then surely there must be a bad disease that led to it.

Indicators are precursors of results. We can't have bad indicators and a good result. We can't have increased troponins and wish that the heart is normal.

When the indicators are bad the result will be bad. And right now the indicators are quite bad.

Global economy is global destiny.

The precision of the universe is at play.

Forget the community; forget the climate; forget the have nots. Let's just achieve targets.

"Ha.Ha."

Nature and Humaneness will together have the last laugh.

"Ha.Ha."

Average Americans have not been saving enough. The haves have it and the have not's do not have it. The gap between them is wide.

Government may be the reason for the recession? Because they bailed out the big banks with public money. And big banks created a speculative bubble of derivates 30 times the size of the US debt – more than $ 500 trillion of derivatives.

Did we talk about executives who own islands while there are millions who can barely rent a shelter.

The haves and the have nots. Is this all about this?

But there is much more to Trump if nearly half of America has voted for someone against distinguished rivals. Trump must surely have touched the core of peoples' aspirations. No doubt.

Lots of people not employed. Lots of people with less salary. Lots of people with less savings. Lots of people with more expenses. Lots of people on the other side. Lots of have nots. USA Today. They have elected Trump. They are watching Trump. He better do something great.

Sometimes it seems like Trump may be the only one who was ever capable of taking the bull by the horns.

The initial pages are the honeymoon days. We all know what happens in the later part of a marriage. The next page – Experience marriage: raw and hard core.

If not for anything just for the high PE get out of US stocks by Sep -2017.

It's not Trump. It's a trumpet.

All talk and no output makes Jack a Trump.

Trump cannot pass bills. Government business will be at standstill.

USA will be caught in the crossfire between Trump, his own party non-supporters, opposition party and the Fed.

Will USA survive Trump?

Will an already divided USA come together again?

The trade war it will be the last nail in the coffin.

Will we be the destined witness of an Economic Downswing?

The Last Quarter Of 2017...Oct 2017. The Downswing Starts.

Sometimes the best comes out of the worst. Hope that we are in that situation.

What we have been doing is against humanity's target. And there lies the crux of the problem and the biggest lesson the Cosmos is trying to teach us though the coming crash.

It is nature's way of purging excess and dead sloth greed from its system. Nature and the real economy don't like these. Small relief.

There is Life beyond ROI.

A must read for everyone to know how the global economy arrived at the mess it is in.

A small spark starts a jungle fire when the twigs are dry and many.

The precision of the universe is at play.

Forget the community; forget the climate; forget the have nots. Let's just achieve targets.

"Ha.Ha."

Nature and Humaneness will together have the last laugh.

"Ha.Ha."

Basically it is about the basics. Basics are the foundation. Basics are the building blocks. Basics are all there is. Basic is the end point.

You get the basic right you get everything right.

You decide your future at the time you act.

Useful plus Used = Effective.

Utilize every moment. These will never come back.

Moments are all you have.

The next two years will reveal that utility is linked to survival.

Charles Darwin's Survival of the Fittest will be successfully tested once again.

Someone who is skilled is always of value. Those who are useful will be used. And will be paid for the use.

Even in a recession people will visit a restaurant that serves tasty nutritious food, to watch that movie which is entertaining and go to that doctor who gives accurate diagnosis.

Compact: This will make a strong comeback.

Compact and utility will go hand in hand.

Warren Buffet has a name for derivatives. He calls them Weapons of Mass Destruction.

There have been 33 recessions in the history of capitalism. The longest expansion has lasted 10 years and the average duration of an expansion is 5 years. We are currently running 10 years.

We are due for the next one between 2019-2020. Maybe late 2018 when Trump would be reassessed by corporate America and the rest of the world?

Will it be the failure of Trump policies or the end of ECB QE that will trigger a domino effect on an already weak Euro - Japan - South American geography? Or will it be the crash of the bad Euro banks that will pull in Japan and USA.

Or will there be a few more Toshiba Nuclear that will one day reveal they are no more. Maybe derivates will again play havoc. Deutsche bank?

To escape the effects of the 2008 QE was started. Pump in easy money. With no real demand.

By not withdrawing QE and taking their medicine in 2012 – market imbalances today are now bigger and the consequences greater.

The culprits are the central banks (though they are not the only ones). This is where they started giving cash to create the cash illusion.

1929. Let's go back and take a look.

In the great depression of 1929 were there no rich people. Yet for every wealthy guy every there were thousands holding the food bowl.

In Venezuela 73 murders occur every day. No investigations.

Money in your hand turns to gas by the time you reach home. Hyperinflation.

Money loses value by the milli second.

 It has among the richest source of oil in the world. What went wrong?

Tens of millions lined up to flee the country.

Not 1929.   In 2019.

Where do you want to be in 2019. How to get to where you want to be in 2019.

Make a decision based on facts. Take a considered opinion.

Belongingness gives us the strength to carry on against all odds. The more we enlarge our belongingness the more humane we will be.

It's a game. The game is on. It can affect. It's real. Play it well. It is not static.

Be alert.

Situations will be dynamic.

Spend at least 10 mins a day to watch targeted news.

Hobby. We can discover facets to life hitherto hidden. That can be fascinating. And you can be the Charles Darrow of 2019!

Forest – Nature. We can discover facets to life hitherto hidden. That can be fascinating.

Follow the legends.

George Soros is in Bear Camp, Jim Roger stays away, Buffet has cash enough to fill a sea.

Cash is king. Cash is Queen. Cash is everythin' Bye - Bye Stock

Accumulate the safe haven metals on dips. Lithium and Cobalt are the new and spectacular 'precious metal' and on the other end is gold the perennial safe haven. Consider graphene – the new kid on the block.

Focus on South Asian funds

Immigrate to happy countries

Reach out to me.

More millionaires were made due to the great depression than at other times.

Happiness is a byproduct of attitude. Improve your attitude.

One step in the right direction gives the strength for two steps in the right direction. Two steps in the right direction gives the strength for 4 steps in the right direction. 4 steps... Just substitute the word right with wrong and see where you end up.

Economy will now have to be managed with an eye on cause and effect.

Whatever we do will comeback to us with a multiplier.

Are we just pumping money (QE) into the system. What are the actual effects? Are the actions of the central banks the answer to combat the 2008 recession or was it just a patch up to leave us vulnerable to bigger disasters. We will know in the coming 2 years. If this is the way to manage a recession then recessions can be managed. We would have devised a mechanism. But if it pans out like more than a few are predicting that this might lead to bigger problems and bigger downturns, then we have to rethink. If we have a chance to rethink, that is.

Whatever we do will comeback to us with a multiplier.

Imagine the time when there were no cities. We lived in the forest. We lived.

When Greece collapsed the banks in Greece were closed. People had to line up at ATMs for their daily ration of fixed money.

A survivor said: Parents dream for their kids. I live a nightmare and see my children foraging garbage for food.

Stay at the fringe of a forest where the city ends. And the recession can be an adventure in a tree house. And you can live.

Get the best of air, water and fruits and enter the city to do what you have to do. But come back to the fringe where the city meets the forest. For this is the place where ... you can live.

You won't need electricity because the moonlight will be there to take care of you and all that you wear.

THE QUOTES

"I think we're in an extremely unsafe (economic) world — we've never been here before." The former director of the Office of Management and Budget, Stockman. Stockman has been a lynchpin of the US government during its heydays.

"A lot of the problems in the investment bank have been that people have been trying to generate revenue at all costs." Thiam, CEO Credit Suisse.

Generate revenue at any cost. "Ha Ha."- The Bears In 2019.

Just in the course of a day the monster of the Dow became a darling of the Dow.

Between Trump, the Fed and the Senate I get an image of a mashed potato .

Europe Lives In Delusion

"A bad bank in Europe? Ah! Tell me something excitin'."

In 2019 economics will make history.

The center of gravity will start to shift to the East.

East Ho ! West No !

175 Global CIO and PM Survey – 2017

Protectionist policies could be the catalyst that may be the end of the 8-year global equity bull market. This is a BofA-ML's latest monthly survey of 175 global chief investment officers and portfolio managers. They together manage $543 billion in assets and this is their opinion.

Trade Wars: 34%
High Interest Rates: 28%
Unpredictable Financial Event: 18%
Weak Earning: 18%

Thirty four percent felt it would be the trade wars while Twenty eight per cent felt that higher interest rates could bring back the bears.

EM equities found favor with global funds. 49 per cent of them said EM equities were undervalued (so we need to head to the emerging markets). So there we have it from the horses' mouth.

I had a bit cosmos hugging me today. Looking at me with limpid eyes. I was carrying her. She will save me from the harsh world. My 2 year girl going onto 3.

The LAST WORD

It will start with the interest rate hike. Stocks will crash. Real estate will join in.

It will start when the QE ends.

It will start with the Euro banks. Taking down Italy, Greece spreading like a contagion through Europe, Japan. USA has its own set of issues that are enough and interconnected for it to fall like never before.

Or is it a war like situation - the South China sea, the aggressive bans polarizing a community, providing fodder for spread of more radical sentiments or is it the renegades that will spook the world.

Is a Depression staring at us never before witnessed in the history of humans. Or is it just a major correction?

The Trump policies have sent Dow on a record high and corporate America is still gung ho.

Investment today is not less than a war.

The Dow keeps breaking records. And the best time to book profits is already past us. That happened when Trump announced the tax breaks and Dow soared. That was best time in a long time the best time to book profits. And get away. From then on it would be performance and not hope that would guide Dow.

That time is gone.

Coz there is nothing to hope for; all the hopes have disappeared. And there seems to be just gloom and doom head.

If you have now have a trade deal euphoria in early 2019 then that might be the last chance get out. It might just be the last chance to get out of the stock market.

Trump on Trump Policy
10-year Economic Effect: Plus 1.5% a year
10 - year debt impact : Nil (!!!)
Assumes trade, immigration and regulatory positives.

Tax Policy Center
10 year Economic Growth: -0.5% a year
10 year debt impact: Plus $7 trillion
Factors interest rate hike due to increase in deficit

See, other than Trump himself others are not quite cheerful about his policies. He scores negative on economic impact and adds more to the debt as per the external calculations.

Trump says his policies won't add a penny to the debt.

Hmm. Is it Trump or a trumpet?

It's so easy to win.... After some time.

Huff, huff, Puff , Puff, Powl, Powl.

This one beats all strategies. Coz Investment is a war the Best Strategy is to SCOOT

And we may say it in kinda joke. But we put all the strategies in just one word. Take our advice. Scoot!

Unborn, unused, unusable. Seems more fictional than wicked truth. Unthinkable.

Homes, restaurants, malls, gladiatorial stadia that should have been bustling with vibrant people were mute witness to empty space.

China's ghost cities costed billions – Debt cities.

The boom that never was.

Trump publicly and brashly said stuff that was being spoken in hushed tones. China's trade dealings were as predatory as its land and sea policies

There's a wild Bull in the China Shop. And the finest Ming crockery is at threat of being smashed to pieces.

Maybe it will start with Euro. It's such a mess.

Or Japan nothing' ever happens there ...

Or S America. As empty as a bottle

Maybe the crash will start with USA after all. 21 trillion debt and the interest rates.

What's left?

China.

I knew about that.

Whaa! The whole world... The whole world is gonna crash.

Dumbo! He got it now. Dumbo.

I can nuclear blast anytime.

As in we didn't have enough on our plate already! Mr. One.

What you get depends on how the globe is doing. It's therefore your business to know about the globe.

The book that everyone should read so that they know where they stand.

Because where you stand may not be safe.

The book to guide you through the madness of a Trump presidency.

The book that every economist and any anchor on television should have when they speak about the global economy.

We are humans. We need to share. There is life beyond targets.

The beast visited us in Oct 2019. In Sep 2018 the 30-year Treasury yields started to journey up, just breaking 3.22%. In Oct 2018 we had one of the worst corrections.

Why we need to be afraid? Coz the ECB a'int started yet. Once ECB stops its own QE the bears will have a feast.

In Dec-2018 the ECB will stop its QE and if not in Dec 2018, sometime in 2019 the Fed will increase its interest rate…

THEN THE BEAST WILL BE BACK.

LIKE NEVER BEFORE.

From The Book – The Sign Of The Bear (Xilla C)

TECH SWING

Tech change can swing it.

It's no secret. The age of tech is on the anvil.

Automation will reach levels of analysis. The repetitive data recognition and data entry ask is primitive. Analytical automatons is the expectation. And we already have systems that help diagnose cancers as well as treat. Seated next to a specialist human doctor will be a specialist automaton doctor.

New Technology Breakthrough: New tech is what will change the entire diaspora. It has the power to change the world on its own. Wherever and whatever you can − Be. Not only invest but be part of new technology. You can be not just an investor, you can be a techie or a technopreneur.

New Age Hunt: Hunt for these and different ways to invest in them. This need not be only by way of stocks. Invest your career. Marissa Meyer invested her career in Google as a fresher. Today she is the CEO of Yahoo. AI, robotics, self driven gadgets, smart applications, digital wears.

New Age Metals: Lithium, Cobalt and Graphene. Same story here. Invest in these in any way you can. Right from the companies that mine them to the companies that use them.

AI and robotics are evolving fast, under the radar. Amazon delivers by drones; Budweiser delivers beer with self driven truck; chatbots talk products; Exit formalities in companies, accounts and finance all the way upto disease diagnosis managed by AI. Robots. They will be all over the place from elderly care and surgery to entertainment and being your best buddy. The thrust of an old age cranking economy and the new age transition will present a striking real time change.

It's not only investing money but investing yourself that can make the difference between survival and riding the crest of the gigantic waves of witnessed historical time transition.

2022- A wave. Flying cars, self driving cars, hyperloop, IOT and global cloud, drones, chatbots, AI, robotics – robot friend, robot butler, robot medic, root surgeon, robot singer, robot actor, robot, robot, robot.

Surf the technology wave.

WHEN IT DOES REVIVE

AS IT WILL

THE

CATACLYSMIC CHANGES

WILL BE

AKIN

TO THE

METAMORPHOSIS

07 A

CATERPILLAR INTO A BUTTERFLY.

In the early 1900 those who were affluent had iceboxes. A horse drawn carriage would stop by to deliver ice everyday. Until refrigerators were invented. Not long back the night was lit by lamps until electricity was discovered. Civilization changed. Time was when letters took days to reach your feelings to your loved ones. SMS does it in an instant. Reality seems magical.

Our children will live in a world they did not grow up in. Drones, hyperloop speed, personalized gene based medical therapy, anti-ageing, robots, facial recognition, chatbots, flying cars (yes they will come much before self driving cars), third dimension of reality and super-technology that will once again change the screen saver of history and make the world so different than it was ever before.

www.xilla.club

AudioBooks.

To Listen To This Visit Xilla Club

Take Money Outta The Stock Markets

Else The Markets Will Take Money Outta You.

Pig Bull Vs Banana Bear: The Legend Of The First
Bull Bear

Only @ www.xilla.club

AudioBook

Stockmarket Drama Video

Europe is as brittle as an old woman's grey hair.

We saw through China.

We are now yellin':

Europe is as brittle as an old woman's grey hair.

Europe is as brittle as an old woman's grey hair.

Europe is as brittle as an old woman's grey hair.

From:

Pig Bull Vs Banana Bear: The Legend Of The First Bull Bear

AudioBook

Stockmarket Drama Video

www.ingramcontent.com/pod-product-compliance
Lightning Source LLC
Chambersburg PA
CBHW030542220526
45463CB00007B/2949